ZOOM  IN

Wake up sleepy-heads!

I'm Nav the alien and I'd like to welcome you to *Zoom In!*
It's time to open those peepers because this edition of
The Navigator is all about looking at things and finding things
out from them. Thanks to the hard work of our roving reporters,
I'll be showing you some wonderful sights on your lovely planet.
I'll also take you to my home, outer space. On your adventures
you'll learn how to make animal shadows, and you'll also meet
some of my fellow aliens in a groovy galactic guessing game.
I bet you didn't know looking at things could be so much fun.

Seeing is believing!

Text Type	Literacy Skills	Wider Curriculum Links
Letter: Recount	Inferential reading; expressing and justifying opinions	**Geography** Unit 7: Weather around the world
Report	Reasoning; deduction; justification; communicating decisions to others	**History** Unit 6C: A Viking case study
Instructional	Close reading; linking text and visuals; deduction	**Science** Unit 3F: Light and shadows
Reference (visual)	Close reading of information; making comparisons; understanding graphic representations	**Geography** Unit 6: Investigating our local area
Recount (visual)	Close reading of visual information; making comparisons; reading sequentially	**History** Unit 8: The lives of rich and poor people in Tudor times
Report	Information retrieval; classification	**Science** Unit 3D: Rocks and soils
Report (visual)	Asking questions; scanning; reading visual information	**Art and Design** Unit 3A: Portraying relationships
Report	Linking text and visuals; exploring authorial intent	**Design and Technology** Unit 3A: Packaging
Report/ Explanation	Interpreting visual information; making inferences	
Explanation	Deductive comprehension; linking text and visuals; locating information	
Fun spread		
		ICT: Year 3 Schemes of work

When you go on holiday, do you send postcards to your friends or family? Postcards are a quick way of telling your news. What's more, the pictures can show what a place is like.

Here are some holiday postcards. What do they tell you about the people who sent them and the places they visited?

WISH WERE

Dear Ms Wright
It's great here! Got on the bus at 9, here by 10.30. Been on some fantastic rides. Mr Reid got soaked on the log flume. He was not a happy man! He said if it wasn't for your broken leg you'd have been the wet one! We've just had our sandwiches. After lunch we're going to start queuing for The Plunge. Harry won't go on it. Hope you're off your crutches soon. Love class 3W

MEXICHROME

Ms Wright
29 Holmdene Road
Winchester Road
Alresford

Hi kids
Got here safely but it was a long flight. So far we've visited the Great Pyramid and been on a camel (very bumpy). Tomorrow we're off on a trip down the Nile. Picked up some stuff on King Tut for your history topic. It's really hot and Dad's burnt his nose. What's life like at Aunty Sue's? Has she let you help with the milking? Be good! See you soon.
Love M & D xxx

Here are the fronts of the postcards. Can you work out which front goes with which postcard back?

Hi everybody,
Having a great time in spite of the bruises! Snowboarding is pretty tricky. Our instructor reckons I might get the hang of it before I wear out the seat of my ski pants. Yesterday it snowed all day, so went shopping instead. Got some great pressies but you'll have to wait till I get back...
CUL8R!   Jo

LUMICAP
COULEURS NATURELLES

(73) Compagnie des Arts Photomécaniques
Avenue Arago - 91380 Chilly-Mazarin
Reproduction interdite

...0·22·PL...
...MOR...

Class
Brook...
Broc...
SE4 7...
Englan...

DIPLOME
PRESTIGE
DE LA

Dear Granny
We've been here 3 whole days and it's still raining! Dad keeps saying it's going to stop. Mum says he doesn't know what he's talking about. We've been on a donkey ride and to the fair. Kyle was sick everywhere when we got off the Big Dipper. I still haven't won a thing in the amusement arcade.
Love your favourite Granddaughter (ha ha)

— 62 Walnut Road - Chelston, Torquay, Devon TQ2 6HU —
Tel. (0803) 60 59 14

Gran...
The C...
Grimsc...
Bourne, Lincs...

C 87   Printed...

Golden Shield

5

VIKING

Who were the Vikings, and why did they come to Britain?

The Viking people came from the three Scandinavian countries: Denmark, Norway and Sweden. Most of them were farmers, but some were craftsmen or tradesmen. Sailing in longships, they invaded Britain from the late 8th century until the middle of the 11th century AD. The Vikings attacked the local people and stole their land and possessions.

Silver penny

- *Found in East Anglia, England*
- *Made of silver*
- *Has the name 'Saint Edmund' on it*

Shoe

- *Found in York, England*
- *Probably made of cow's leather*
- *Worn by a child*

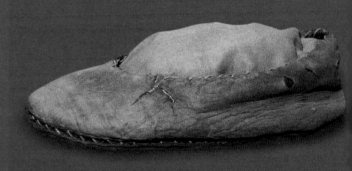

Stirrup

- *Found in the River Witham, Lincolnshire, England*
- *Made of iron and copper*
- *Used by a rich person on their horse's saddle*

Game (King's table)

- *Found in Ballinderry, Ireland*
- *Counters were probably made of glass, ivory or amber*
- *Used for entertainment*

ARTEFACTS

So, how do we know about their culture?

One way of finding out about a culture is to study the artefacts left by the people. In a few places around Britain, excavations have uncovered many interesting items that have helped archaeologists and historians to piece together the lives of the Vikings.

Here are just a few:

Antler comb

- *Found in York, England*
- *Made of deer or elk horn*
- *Used by all members of society*

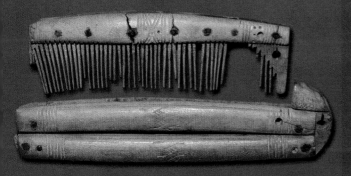

Brooch

- *Found in Orkney, Scotland*
- *Made of silver*
- *Used to fasten men's cloaks*

Swords

- *Found in Dublin, Ireland*
- *Made of iron*
- *Used by a warrior for fighting*

Lewis chessmen

- *Found in Lewis, Scotland*
- *Made of walrus tusks*
- *Used for playing chess*

Shadow Play

Shadow Play

A dark room... a bright light... a shadow on the wall. There's an eagle, a dog, a beautiful swan...

Have you ever tried making animal shadows? They are fun when you know how. All you need are:
- ★ a bright torch or lamp
- ★ a bare wall
- ★ your hands!

How does it work?

Light always travels in straight lines. When it hits your hands, it can't shine through them, so a shadow forms on the other side.

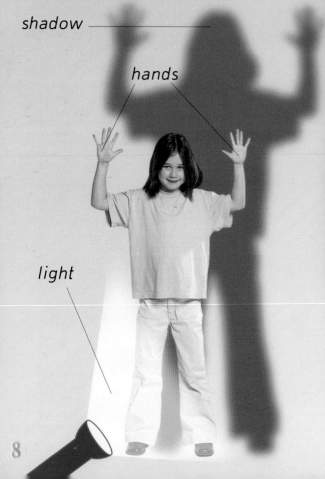

shadow

hands

light

Here are some names for different parts of your hands and arms. You will need to know these words to follow the instructions.

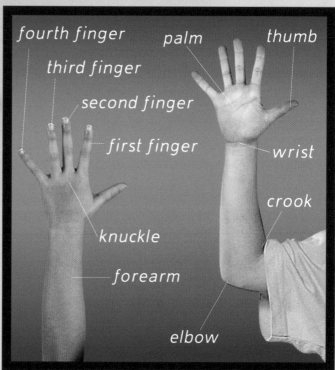

fourth finger
third finger
second finger
first finger
palm
thumb
wrist
crook
knuckle
forearm
elbow

Making shadows

Opposite are three shadows you can make with your hands with step-by-step instructions. But the shadows and the instructions are jumbled up. Can you sort them out?

1. Instruction

1 Put the palms of your hands together with your fingers closed.
2 Make a gap between your thumbs and your first fingers.
3 Make a gap between your third and fourth fingers.
4 Curl in your first fingers so that your knuckles meet.
5 Stretch out your arms.

2. Instruction

1 Cross your hands at your wrists with your palms facing you.
2 Wind your thumbs around each other and press them together.
3 Stretch your fingers up and back, keeping them closed.

3. Instruction

1 Bend your left arm at the elbow with the forearm up straight.
2 Bend your hand at the wrist, keeping the fingers together.
4 Lower your thumb to make a gap.
5 Rest the wrist of your right hand in the crook of the arm.
6 Fan out the fingers of your right hand.

Mystery shadow

Take a look at this mystery shadow. Can you guess what it is? Try to make it with your hands and then write some instructions for it. Ask a friend to test your instructions. Do they really work?

9

Three of a kind

Here are three different views of York: a map (1), an aerial photograh (2), and a 3D drawing (3). Choose some places on the map, then find them in the photograph and drawing. Then, find some streets in the photograph and the drawing, and find their names on the map!

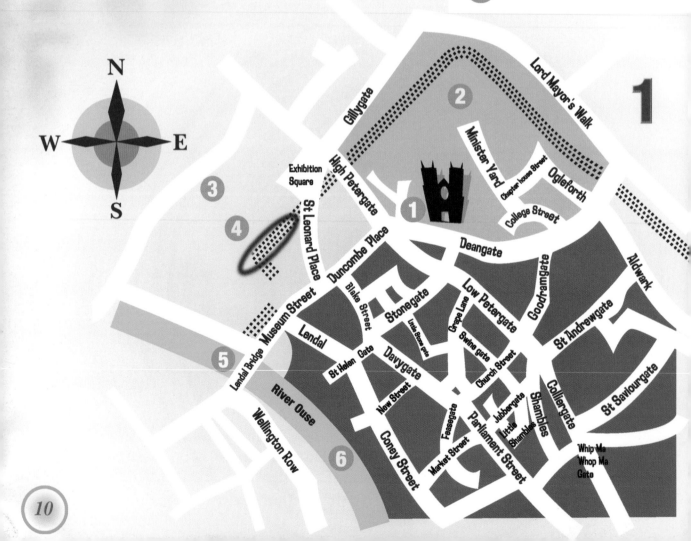

2

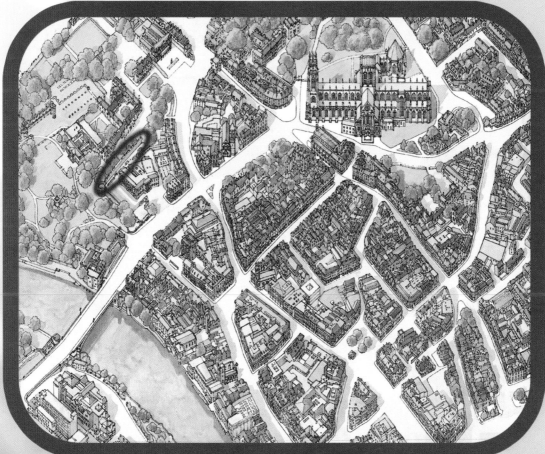

3

A DAY IN THE LIFE ...

6 am 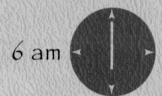   10 am 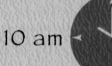   midday

What was it like to be a child in Tudor England? Life was very different for rich and poor people. All children were brought up to live the same sort of lives as their parents, from kings to farmers. Let's take a look at one day in the life of a poor child and a rich child in late August, 1580.

3 pm   6 pm   9 pm

ROCK ON!

A guide to the world's most remarkable rocks

Miners dig it. Builders build with it. Children bang their knees on it. What is it? ROCK!

Rock can be chipped and shaped in all sorts of ways. The rocks below have remarkable shapes. How were they formed?

Each picture has a clue that shows how big the rock is. Can you spot them?

THE GIANT'S CAUSEWAY

Place: County Antrim, Northern Ireland
Description: 40 000 columns of rock
Made of: Basalt
How formed: Hot rock flowed out from inside the Earth, and cracked into columns as it cooled.
Extra info: Most of the columns have five sides.

WHITE HORSE OF UFFINGTON

Place: Oxfordshire, UK
Description: Large figure of a horse cut into the hillside
Made of: Chalk
How formed: People cut away the topsoil, showing the white chalky rock below.
Extra info: The figure could be over 2300 years old. It may have been carved as a gift to Epona, the Roman goddess of horses.

GAPING GILL

Place: Yorkshire, UK
Description: Huge underground cave
Made of: Limestone
How formed: An underground river wore away the rock.
Extra info: This is the largest limestone cave in the country.

ULURU

Place: Northern Territory, Australia
Description: Huge hill in the desert
Made of: Sandstone
How formed: It was once a larger mountain, but it has been worn away by wind and water.
Extra info: Uluru used to be known as "Ayer's Rock".
There are many large caves in the rock. Some of them contain ancient wall paintings.
Uluru appears to change colour in different lights.

RAINBOW BRIDGE

Place: Utah, USA
Description: The world's largest natural bridge
Made of: Sandstone
How formed: A river carved an opening through the rock.
Extra info: The bridge could span a football pitch – it is 84 metres wide.

MOUNT RUSHMORE

Place: South Dakota, USA
Description: Huge sculpture of four US presidents
Made of: Granite
How formed: The sculpture was cut into the rock by over 400 workers.
Extra info: This is the world's largest sculpture. It took fourteen years to make, and was completed in 1941.
The faces are 21 metres high. The eyes are over three metres wide, the noses are six metres long, and the mouths are over five metres long.

15

GUESS THE ALIEN!

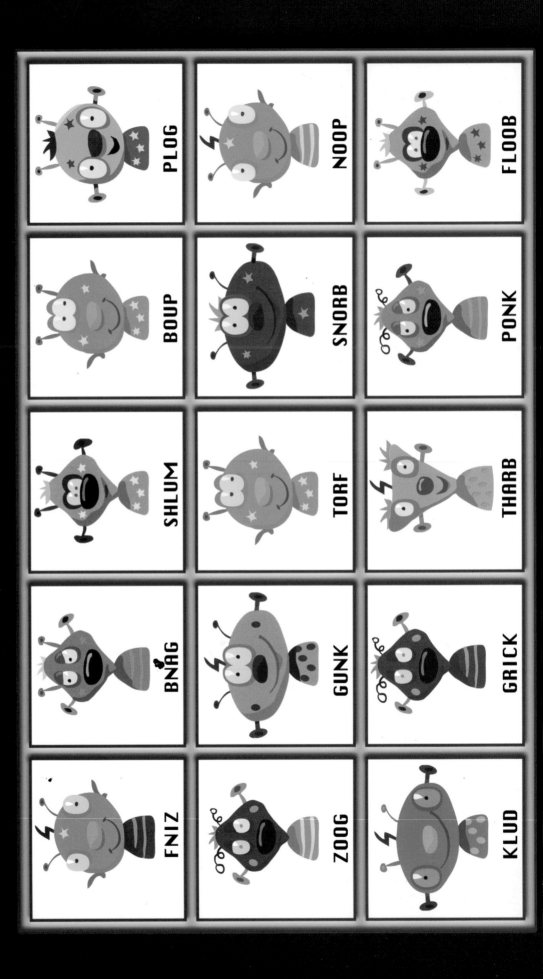

PLOG

NOOP

FLOOB

BOUP

SNORB

PONK

SHLUM

TORF

THARB

BNAG

GUNK

GRICK

FNIZ

ZOOG

KLUD

16

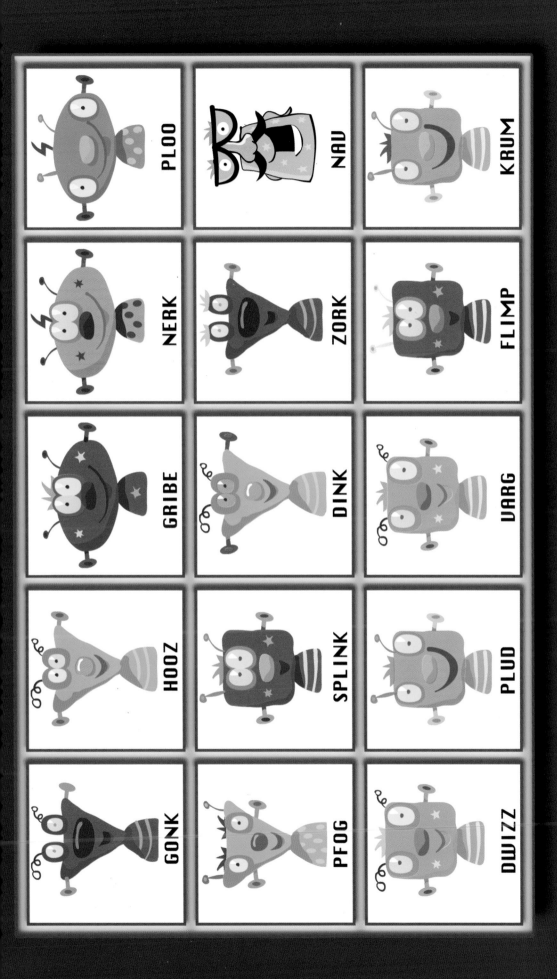

The aliens have landed! But they all look very similar.
Can you tell who's who?

We don't often think about packaging. But just imagine what life would be like without it.

Take tea. Tea comes in bags and packets. Take fizzy drinks. Fizzy drinks come in bottles and cans. Take crisps. Crisps come in bags. Take human beings. Yes, even we are packaged – in skin. Imagine what we'd be like without our packaging. Eeeergh!

Most packaging is very sensible. But not all. Some is mind-bogglingly, round-the-twist bonkers! Here are a few products whose packaging could definitely be improved:

Milk. The kind that comes in cartons. You carefully read the instructions telling you how to open the carton, then – sploosh! You spend the next five minutes drying the cat with a towel.

Beetroot, marmalade, jams (almost anything in jars). The lids on some of these are so tight you need to do a body-building course to open them.

PACKAGING

Cereals. "To open, slide finger under flap", it says on the box. You do as you're told – and either cut your finger or tear the flap. Then you try to open the tightly sealed packet inside. To do this, you have to rip it apart. Cereal flies everywhere. Finally you follow the instruction to slip the little tab on top of the box into the little slit on the opposite flap. The little slit refuses to open. You throw the packet on the floor and jump on it.

Toothbrushes. New toothbrushes often come in plastic casing so tough and hard that you need to call the fire brigade to get into it.

Have you ever had problems with packaging? How could things be improved?

Out of this world!

RUDDER
The rudder helps the shuttle steer.

What is a space shuttle?

A space shuttle is a spacecraft that is sent into orbit around the Earth. It is used to launch or repair satellites in space. Space shuttles are also being used to build NASA's new International Space Station. Shuttles are able to return to Earth and can be used over and over again.

USA

MAIN ENGINE
The main engine thrusts the shuttle off the ground and into space.

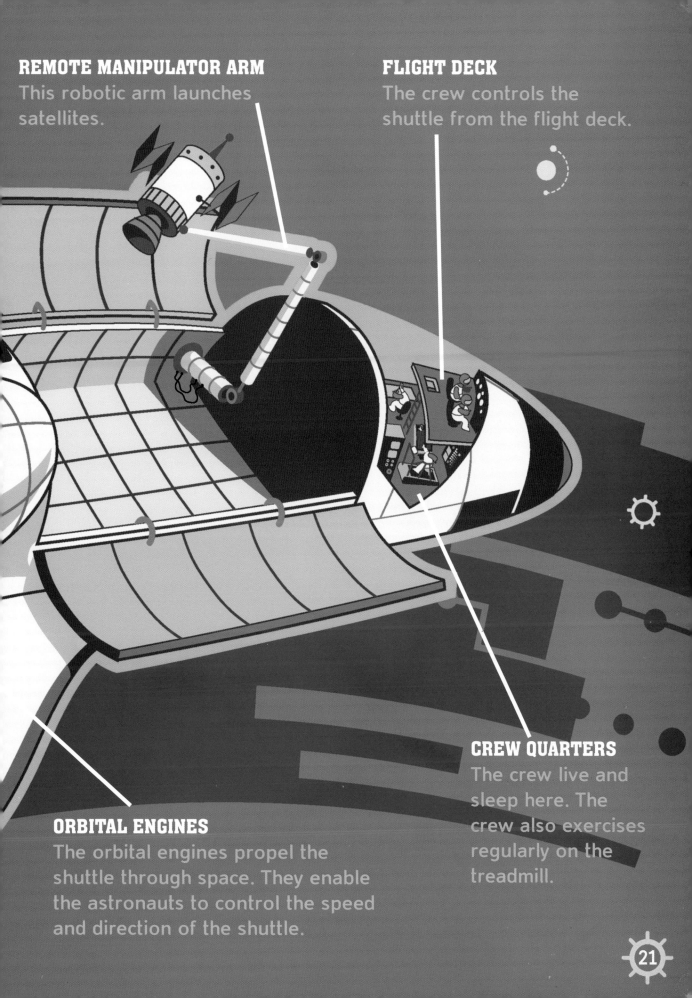

REMOTE MANIPULATOR ARM
This robotic arm launches satellites.

FLIGHT DECK
The crew controls the shuttle from the flight deck.

ORBITAL ENGINES
The orbital engines propel the shuttle through space. They enable the astronauts to control the speed and direction of the shuttle.

CREW QUARTERS
The crew live and sleep here. The crew also exercises regularly on the treadmill.

LIGHTS, CAMERA, SPECIAL EFFECTS!

SPECIAL EFFECTS IN FILMS

A giant chicken is stalking the streets … Terrifying waves threaten a tiny boat … A scary face jumps out at you from the screen. Have you ever wondered how they do that? It's all down to special effects. Special effects is the art of creating pictures and sounds that seem real on the screen. Read on to find out how some of these special effects are created and used in films.

GREEN-SCREEN PHOTOGRAPHY

It's not always possible to film actors or animals in the right setting, especially when they have to look larger than life. Take this chicken, for example. First it is filmed in front of a green screen. The image of the chicken is then separated from the green and projected onto some background scenery. Both images are filmed life-size, but when they are combined, the chicken looks huge!

ANIMATRONICS

Animatronics is a type of special effect that creates life-like robots. These could be animals, people, or even aliens. A special effects crew uses remote control to make the robots move. Because animatronic creatures seem to move like living creatures, they can be filmed alongside actors.

WEATHER EFFECTS

Special effects are often used in films to create weather conditions and natural disasters. For example, to film a boat caught in a violent storm at sea, actors can sit safely in a boat in a large tank in a studio. A machine creates crashing waves in the water, fans produce powerful winds, and giant overhead sprinklers send down pounding rain. The scene is filmed in front of a plain coloured screen. It is then combined with a real or computer-generated seascape.

MAKE-UP TRICKERY

Film make-up artists can turn actors into monsters or alien creatures. They can make young people look old, or make actors appear as if they have been in horrible accidents. Thin layers of a type of rubber called latex are often used to create artificial skin. Each layer must dry before the next is added. This means that some actors have to be in make-up for several hours before each day's filming!

CLOSE CALLS

What do these photographs show? Here's a clue: they are all close-up views of common, everyday objects. Can you work out what they are? Check the answers at the bottom of the page.

1

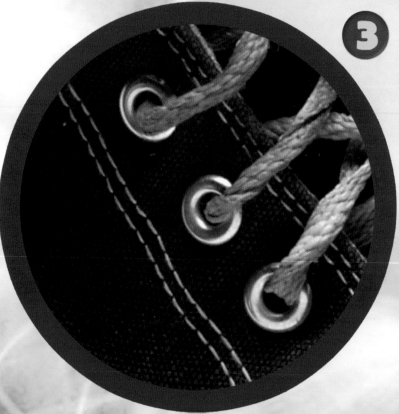

2

3

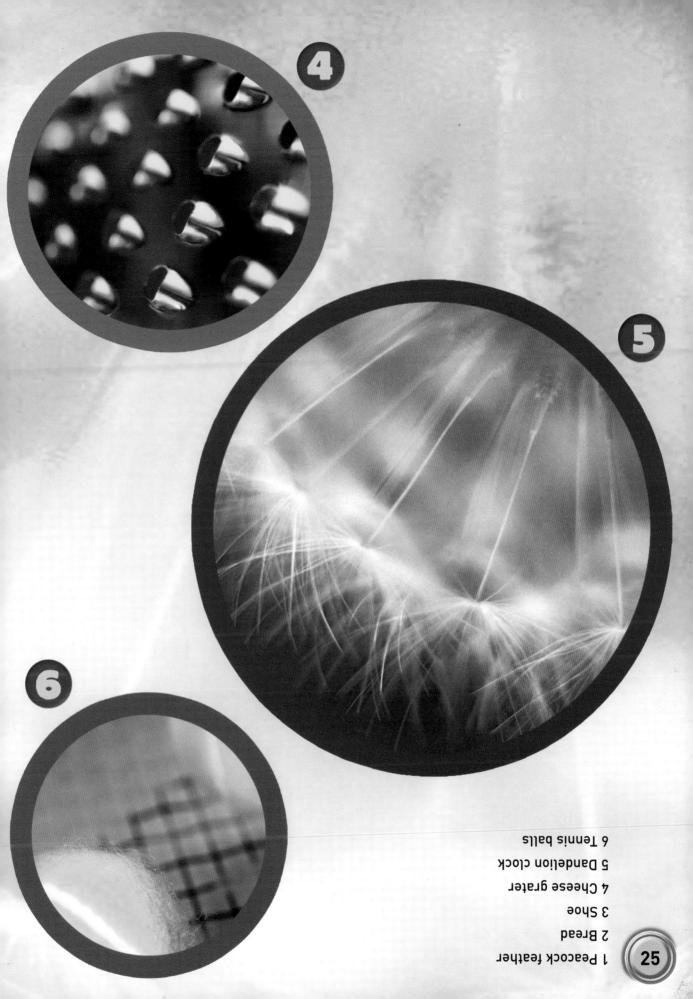

25

Byte-Sized ICT

Wish you were here?

Website visits

Using the Internet is a great way to find out about places you plan to visit, before you go. Many theme parks, museums and wildlife parks, as well as towns and cities, have their own websites. Try searching for somewhere you would like to see, then find three reasons that make you want to go!

Helpful hint!

To find the website for a place to visit, try typing the name then **.co.uk** or **.com**

Close calls

ICT: Unit 3a
Resizing graphics

Classroom close-up

Why not use a digital camera to take some close-up photographs of objects in the classroom. Before you print them out, use the 'crop' button to cut away some of the picture. Leave one small section. You could enlarge the picture too. Can a friend guess what it is?

If you don't have a digital camera, your computer may have some clip-art photos to use.

This is the crop button

Bad packaging

ICT: Unit 3a
Combining text and graphics

Design a wrapper

A paint program is a great way of designing your own packaging. Try creating a wrapper for a new healthy snack bar. First think of a name, then think of what you could put on the wrapper to go with the name. There are some cool tools in paint programs to help you – all sorts of shapes, colours and effects. Have fun trying them out!

Don't forget *to include some notes with your design about how the packaging will work. You could even print it out and try making it with paper.*

Lights, camera, special effects!

ICT: Unit 3a

Using different fonts, etc.

Film fun

With so many special effects now possible, film writers can include almost anything they can think of in their films, however weird or wonderful!

Have a go at thinking of your own unusual character, creature or event to feature in a fantastic film, using lots of special effects. Type a short description of it on the computer. Then use a different font or italics to type some details of the special effects you would use.

A day in the life...

ICT: Unit 3a

Using different fonts, etc.

Different Days

Look closely at the pictures in this article. How many differences can you find between the life of a poor child and the life of a rich child in Tudor times? Type a list, using a different colour for rich and poor. For example:

Poor children had to work.

Rich children were taught lessons.

When you have finished, look at your list. How many differences did you find? If you were alive in Tudor times, which would you rather be – rich or poor?

Viking artefacts

Viking longship research challenge

Can you find out what a Viking longship looked like?
You could do a search on a CD-ROM encyclopedia, a history
CD-ROM or the Internet. If possible, try to print out a picture
of a longship.

Helpful hint!

When you're searching for
something, you may need to
type in different words to do
with Viking longships, such
as *Vikings, longships, boats,
ships, travel.*

Glossary

amusement arcade	a place where a number of electronic games are situated
animatronics	making and operating lifelike robots, typically for use in film
archeologist	a person who studies ancient cultures by digging up and examining things they have left behind, such as buildings, pots or coins
artefacts	objects made by humans, such as tools or works of art
crew	the people who work on a ship or aircraft
King Tutankhamun (Tut)	Egyptian Pharaoh, who reigned between c.1361 – c.1352 BC
lift-off	the rising off the ground or launch pad of an aircraft, spacecraft or helicopter
light	the radiation from the sun, a fire or some similar source that lets us see things

River Nile	a river in eastern Egypt
rock	a large stone or mass of stone
satellite	an object sent into space to orbit around the Earth or another planet. It gathers and sends back information
Scandanavian	from the countries of Norway, Sweden and Denmark
snowboarding	skiing with a single, wide ski
Tudor	the period of history between 1485 and 1603
Vikings	sailors from Norway, Sweden and Denmark who raided and traded with people in north-west Europe between the 8th and 11th centuries

Index